by Kris Bonnell

Corn grows from a corn seed.

This is an ear of corn.

A cob is inside an ear of corn.

Here is some corn on the cob.

Here is some corn off the cob.

We eat corn.

We make food out of corn.

Most of the corn
that we eat is yellow.
Corn can also be red, brown,
black or white.

Animals eat corn.
We do not eat
the kind of corn
that animals eat.

If this kind of corn is cooked, it will become...

POPCORN!

We can eat popcorn!